PIANO+VOCAL+GUITAR

THE BEST OF MODERN WORSHIP

WORSHIP TOGETHER

HERE I AM to WORSHIP 2

ISBN 0-634-09857-8

HAL•LEONARD® CORPORATION
7777 W. BLUEMOUND RD. P.O. BOX 13819 MILWAUKEE, WI 53213

For all works contained herein:
Unauthorized copying, arranging, adapting, recording or public performance is an infringement of copyright.
Infringers are liable under the law.

Visit Hal Leonard Online at
www.halleonard.com

CONTENTS

Title	Page	Artist
As I Lift You Up	4	**Jeff Deyo**
Be Near	10	**Shane & Shane**
Better Is One Day	26	**Kutless**
Blessed Be Your Name	19	**Tree63**
Consuming Fire	32	**Tim Hughes**
Facedown	40	**Matt Redman**
Filled With Your Glory	46	**Starfield**
Glory	53	**Johnny Parks**
Grace Like Rain	62	**Todd Agnew**
He Reigns	71	**Newsboys**
Here I Am To Worship	78	**Phillips, Craig and Dean**
Living Hallelujah	84	**Sarah Kelly**
Lost In Wonder	92	**Martyn Layzell**
No One Like You	108	**David Crowder*Band**
Rain Down	116	**Delirious?**
Salvation	126	**Charlie Hall**
Sing To The King	132	**Passion Band**
Song Of Love	136	**Rebecca St. James**
Spirit	99	**Switchfoot**
Spirit Waltz	142	**Something Like Silas**
Stronger Than The Storm	152	**Vicky Beeching**
Take My Life	147	**Chris Tomlin**
We Bow Down	160	**Twila Paris**
Wonderful Maker	166	**Jeremy Camp**
Yahweh	172	**Shawn McDonald**

AS I LIFT YOU UP

Words and Music by
JEFF DEYO

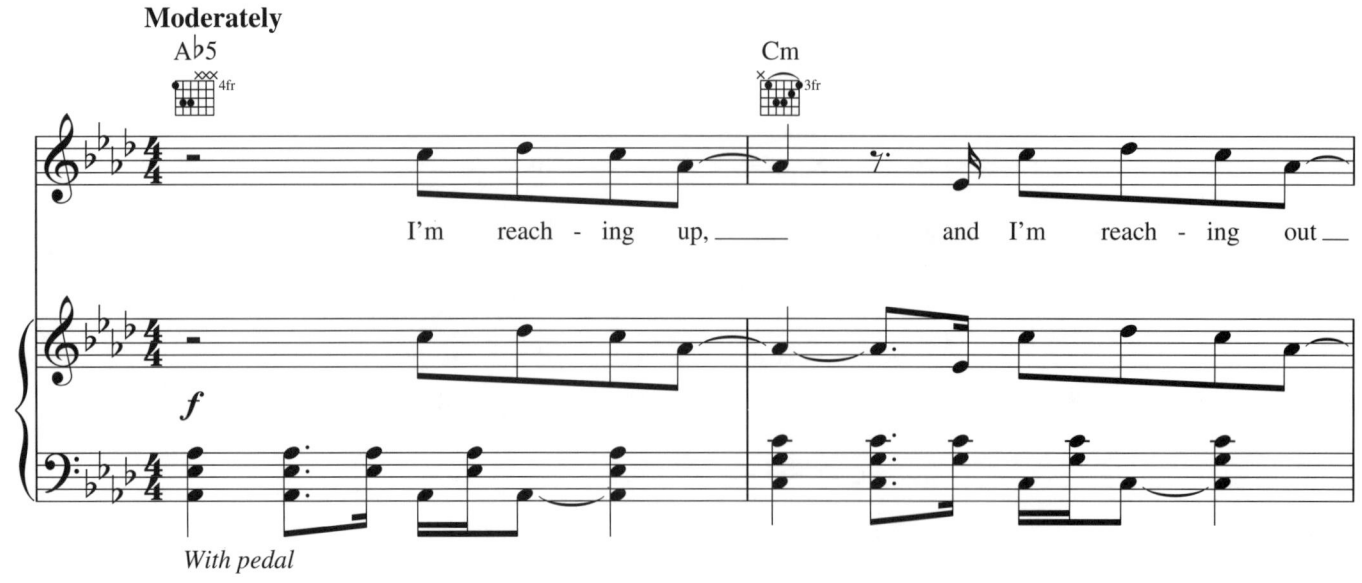

I'm reach-ing up, and I'm reach-ing out to be with You, Lord; I wan-na be with You now. There's noth-ing quite like Your voice in my ear; it's gen-tle and soft, you know, it's hon-est and real.

© 2003 EMACK MUSIC (ASCAP) and WORSHIP CITY MUSIC (ASCAP)
Admin. by EMI CMG PUBLISHING
All Rights Reserved   Used by Permission

(Da da da da, da da da da, da da da da, da da, da da.)

If it is true, then how can it be: The thing You want most from me is in-ti-ma-cy?

I try in my pow'r to give You e-nough; but first what You ask

call ev-'ry-one to Your throne? Won't You call ev-'ry-one to Your throne? Come make me all that You want me to be, my prais-es work-ing that all would be-lieve. Change us for all of e-ter-ni-ty. As I lift You up from the earth, won't You

BE NEAR

Words and Music by
SHANE BARNARD

© 2003 RIVER OAKS MUSIC COMPANY (BMI), TRUE BLISS MUSIC (BMI) and WAITING ROOM MUSIC (BMI)
Admin. by EMI CMG PUBLISHING
All Rights Reserved   Used by Permission

CONSUMING FIRE

Words and Music by
TIM HUGHES

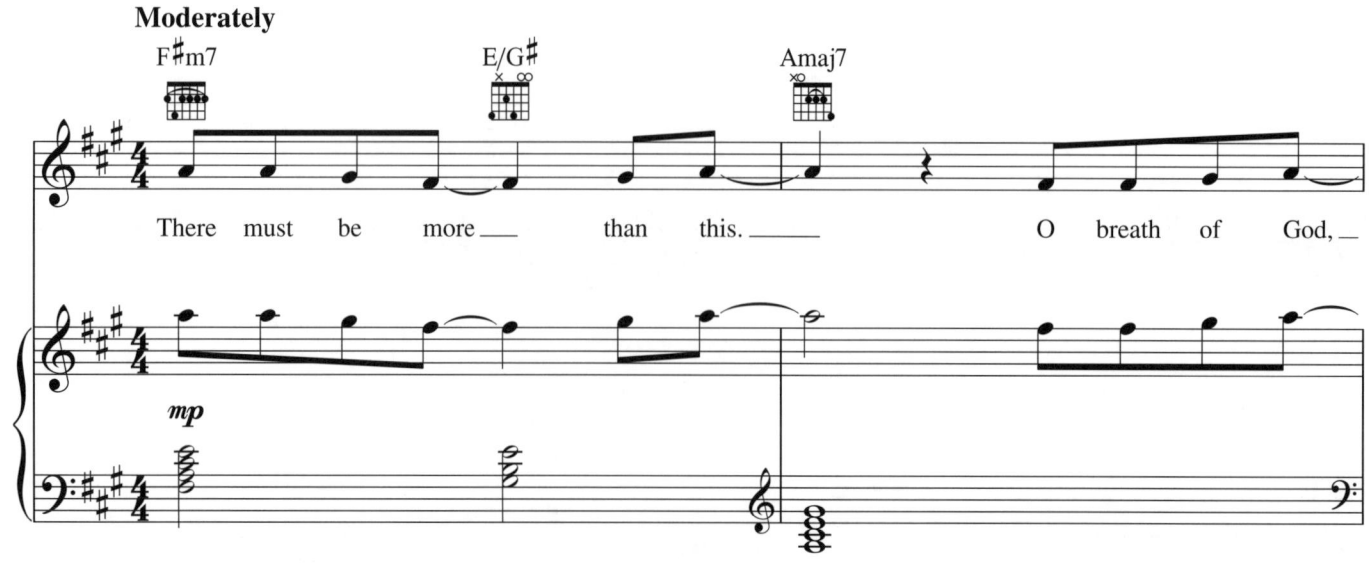

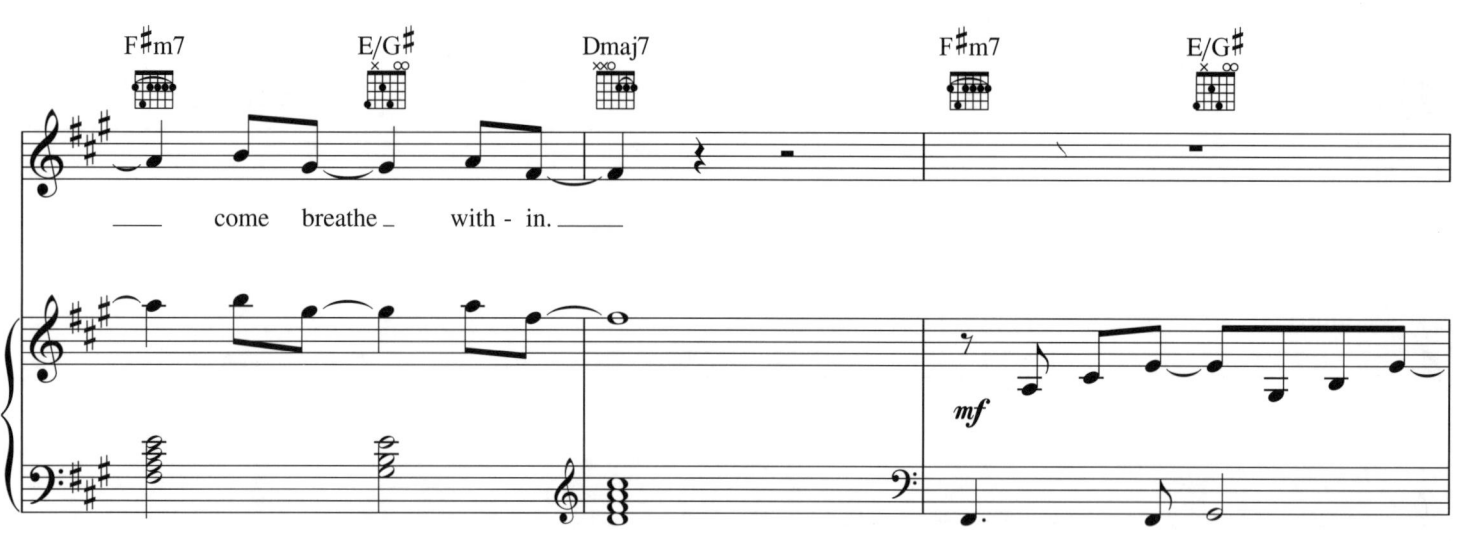

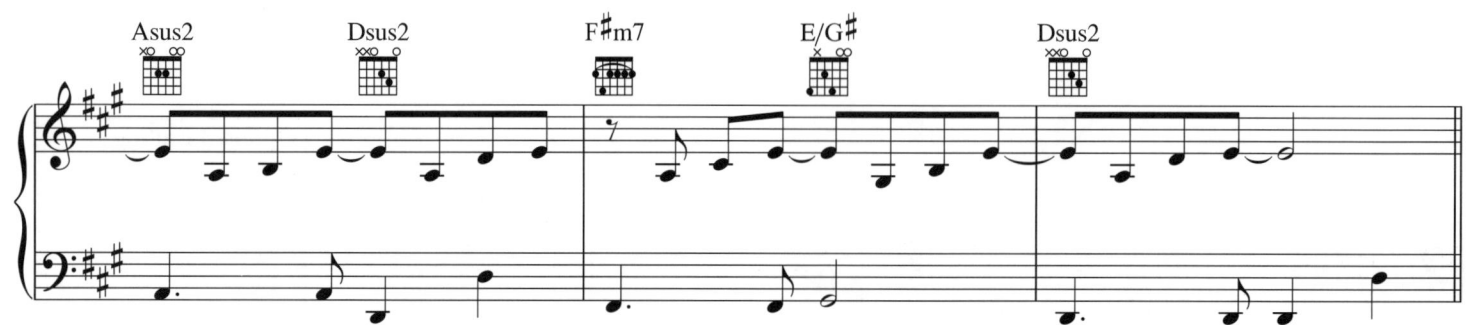

© 2002 THANKYOU MUSIC (PRS)
Admin. Worldwide excluding the UK and Europe by WORSHIPTOGETHER.COM SONGS
Admin. in the UK and Europe by KINGSWAY MUSIC
All Rights Reserved   Used by Permission

_____ more. _____ Con-sum-ing Fire, fan _____ in-to _____ flame _____ a pas-sion for Your name. _____ Spir-it _____ of God, would You fall in _____ this _____ place? Lord, have _____ Your

38

Stir it up in our hearts, Lord. Stir it up in our hearts, Lord.

Stir it up in our hearts, a passion for Your name.

Stir it up in our hearts, Lord. Stir it up in our hearts, Lord.

Stir it up in our hearts, a passion for Your name, O Lord.

FACEDOWN

Words and Music by MATT REDMAN
and BETH REDMAN

Prayerfully

(1.,2.) Welcomed in to the courts of the King, I've been ushered in to Your presence. Lord, I stand on Your merciful ground, yet with ev'ry step tread with rev-'rence.

(3.) Who is there in the heavens like You, and upon the earth who's Your equal? You are far above, You're the highest of heights. We are bowing down to ex-

*Recorded a half step lower.

© 2002 THANKYOU MUSIC (PRS)
Admin. Worldwide excluding the UK and Europe by WORSHIPTOGETHER.COM SONGS
Admin. in the UK and Europe by KINGSWAY MUSIC
All Rights Reserved   Used by Permission

2, 3
Cmaj7
rev - 'rence.
alt You.
And I'll
G(add2)
C
Em7
Dsus
fall face - down as Your glo - ry shines a - round.
C(add2)
G(add2)
C
Yes, I'll fall face - down as Your
Em7
Dsus
To Coda
C(add2)
D.S. al Coda
(take 2nd ending)
glo - ry shines a - round.

CODA
C(add2)
G(add2)
C
Yes, I'll fall face - down as Your
Em7
Dsus
C(add2)
G(add2)
glo - ry shines a - round. God, I'll fall face -
C
Em7
Dsus
C(add2)
down as Your glo - ry shines a - round,
Dsus
C(add2)
Dsus
a - round, a - round.

C(add2)
Dsus
C(add2)
So let Your glo - ry shine a - round, let Your glo - ry shine a - round. King of glo - ry, here be
1, 2
Dsus
found, King of glo - ry.
3
Dsus
found, King of glo - ry.
C(add2)
So let Your glo - ry shine a -
Dsus
C(add2)
Dsus
round, let Your glo - ry shine a - round. King of glo - ry, here be found, King of glo - ry.
C(add2)
Dsus
C(add2)
(Vocal 1st time only)

1
Dsus
2
Dsus
G(add2)
Oh, and I'll fall face -
C
Em7
Dsus
C(add2)
down as Your glo - ry shines a - round.
Yes, I'll
G(add2)
C
1
Em7
Dsus
fall face - down as Your glo - ry shines a - round,
C(add2)
a - round, a - round. God, I'll
2
Em7
Dsus
C(add2)
glo - ry shines a - round.

45

So let Your glory shine a-round, let Your glory shine a-round. King of glory, here be found, King of glory. So let Your glory shine a-round, let Your glory shine a-round. King of glory, here be found, King of glory.

FILLED WITH YOUR GLORY

Words and Music by TIM NEUFELD
and JON NEUFELD

Moderate Rock

In my heart, in my heart, there's a fi-re burning, a pas-sion deep with-in my soul, not slow-ing

of the earth to the heights of Heav-en, Your glo-ry, Lord, is far and wide. Through his-to-

© 2004 BIRDWING MUSIC (ASCAP) and FIELDSTAR MUSIC (ASCAP)
Admin. by EMI CMG PUBLISHING
All Rights Reserved   Used by Permission

down, not grow-ing cold; ____ an un-quench-
ry You reign __ on high. ____ From the depths __

-a-ble flame __ that keeps burn - ing __ bright - er,
__ of the sea __ to the moun - tain's __ sum - mit,

a love that's blaz-ing like __ the sun __
Your pow - er, Lord, it knows __ no bounds. __

for who You are and what __ You've done. __
A high - er love can - not __ be found. __

And as the fire is raging on, so Your praise becomes my song. The whole earth is filled with Your glory, Lord.

So let the universe proclaim Your great pow'r and Your great name.

Angels and men adore; creation longs for what's in store. May You be honored and glorified, exalted and lifted high. Here at Your feet I lay my life.

1
A♭
4fr
A♭sus
4fr
A♭
4fr
A♭sus
4fr
From the ends
2
A♭
4fr
The whole earth is filled with Your glo - ry, Lord.
E♭/G
3fr
E♭
3fr
B♭m11
4fr
Moun - tains bow and o - ceans roar;

creation longs for what's ____ in store. ____ May You be honored and glorified, ____ exalted and lifted high, ____ yeah. ____ Here at __ Your feet I lay ____ my __ life, ____ yeah. ____

Yeah.

GLORY

Words and Music by
JOHNNY PARKS

With a driving beat

God, You are my God.
Death is o - ver - come,

There's no one else like You. You
for - giv - en is my sin.

© 2001 THANKYOU MUSIC (PRS)
Admin. Worldwide excluding the UK and Europe by WORSHIPTOGETHER.COM SONGS
Admin. in the UK and Europe by KINGSWAY MUSIC
All Rights Reserved Used by Permission

glad - ly gave Your blood to bring me back to You.
Heav - en is my home, You wel - come me in.

I will sing Your praise,
I can't wait to hear the

I will lift Your name, I'll glad - ly give You all
saints join in one song, as we praise the lov - ing Son

to see Your king - dom reign.
who's giv - en us His all.
And I won't

be a-shamed when I lift up Your name to let all the world see You are the King. No, I won't be a-shamed when I lift up Your name to let all the world see You are the King. We give You glo - ry, _____ glo - ry ___ to You. ___

We give You glo - ry, _____

glo - ry ___ to You. ___

Glo - ry, glo - ry to You. We give You glo - ry, glo - ry to You.

58

D/F#
Em7
A
up Your name to let all the world see You are the King. No, I won't
G/B
D/A
be a - shamed when I lift up Your name to let all
Em7
A
the world see You are the King. No, I won't
G/B
D/A
be a - shamed when I lift up Your name to let all

the world see You are the King.

We give You glo - ry, glo - ry to You. Glo - ry,

glo - ry __ to You, _____

You, You, __ You, You, You, __ You, You, You, __ You,

You.

GRACE LIKE RAIN

Words and Music by CHRIS COLLINS
and TODD AGNEW

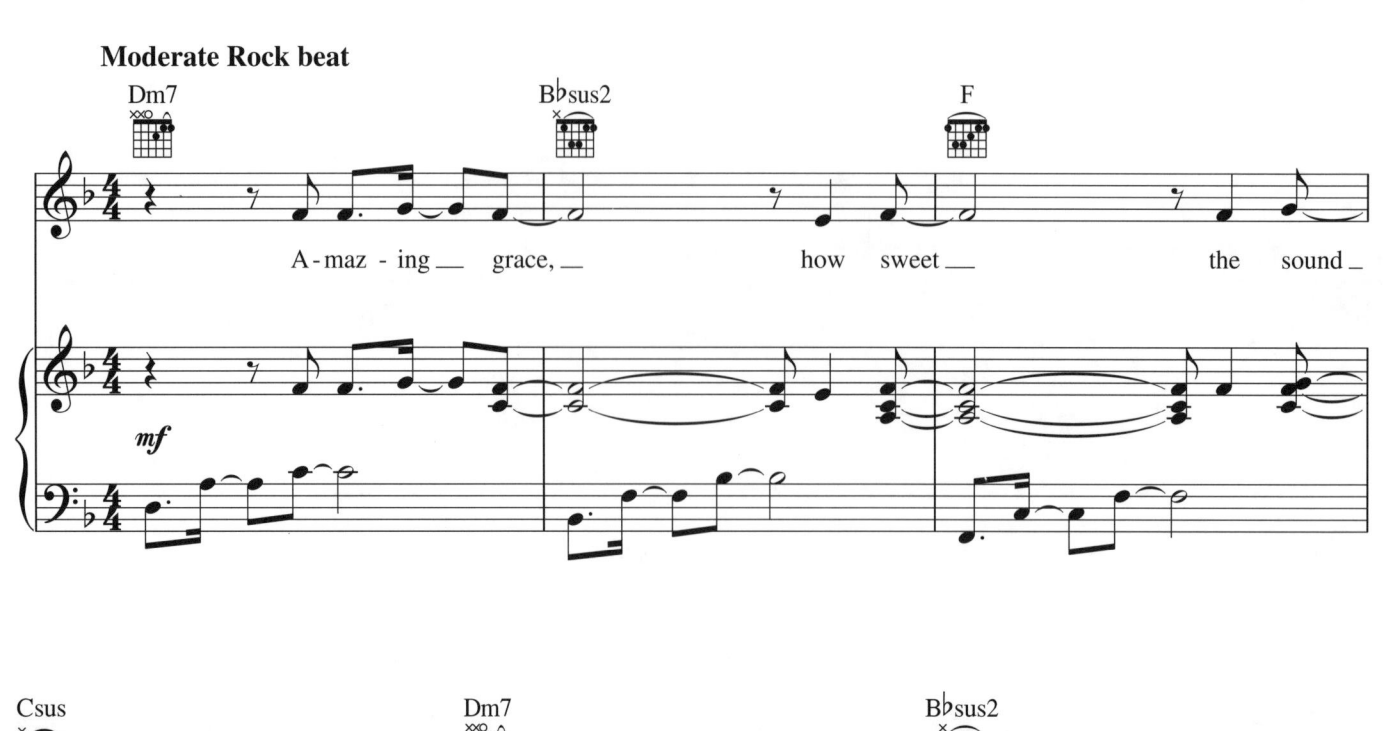

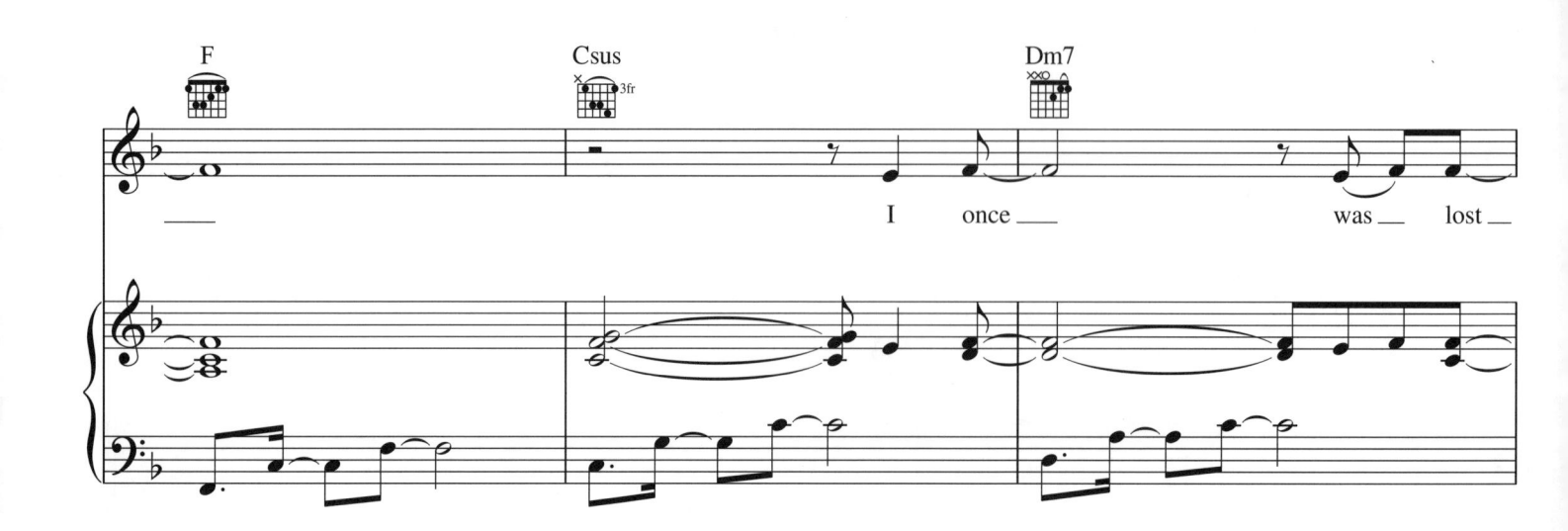

but now __ I'm found; __ Was __ blind __ but now __ I see __ so clear- -ly. __ Hal-le-lu-jah, __ grace like rain falls __ down __ on me. __ Hal-le-lu-

-jah, and all my stains are washed a-way, they're washed a-way.

'Twas grace that taught my heart

to fear, and grace my fears relieved. How precious did that grace appear the hour I first believed.

Hal-le-lu-jah, grace like rain falls down on me. Hal-le-lu-jah, and all my stains are washed a-way, they're washed a-way.

When we've been there ten thou-sand years, bright shin-

-ing as the sun, we've no less days to sing Your praise than when we first be-gun.

69

Hallelujah, grace like rain falls down on me. Hallelujah, and all my stains are washed away.

They're washed away.

Dm7
B♭
F
Hal - le - lu - jah, yeah.
C
Dm7
1
B♭
Hal - le - lu - jah, yeah,
F
C
2
B♭
yeah.
- jah, and all my stains
F
C
N.C.
are washed a - way, they're washed a - way.

HE REIGNS

Words and Music by PETER FURLER and STEVE TAYLOR

Joyfully

It's the
song of the redeemed rising from the African plain.
rise above the four winds, caught up in the heavenly sound.

© 2002 ARIOSE MUSIC (ASCAP) and SOYLENT TUNES (SESAC)
ARIOSE MUSIC Admin. by EMI CMG PUBLISHING
SOYLENT TUNES Admin. by ICG
All Rights Reserved Used by Permission

[G5]

Let prais-es ech-o from the It's the

[F] [C/E]

song of the for-giv-en drown-ing out the Am-a-zon rain.
tow-ers of ca-the-drals to the faith-ful gath-ered un-der-ground.

[G5]

Of all the songs sung from the The song of

[F] [C/E]

A-sian be-liev-ers, filled with God's ho-ly fire.
dawn of cre-a-tion, some were meant to per-sist.

It's ev'ry tribe, ev'ry tongue, ev'ry nation; a love song born of a grateful choir.
Of all the bells rung from a thousand steeples, none rings truer than this.

It's all God's children singing, "Glory, glory, hallelujah! He reigns, He reigns!"

It's all God's chil-dren sing-ing, "Glo-ry, glo-ry, hal-le-lu-jah! He reigns, ___ He reigns." Let it

It's all God's chil-dren sing-ing, "Glo-ry, glo-ry, hal-le-lu-jah! He reigns, ___ He reigns!"

It's all God's children singing, "Glo-ry, glo-ry, hal-le-lu-jah! He reigns, He reigns." And all the pow-ers of dark-ness trem-ble at what they've just heard, 'cause all the powers of darkness can't drown out a single word.

When all God's children sing out, "Glory, glory, hallelujah! He reigns, He reigns!"

All God's { (1.) children sing out, (2.-4.) people singing, } "Glory, glory, hal-le-lu-jah! He reigns, ___ He reigns!" All God's peo-ple sing-ing,

All God's chil-dren sing-ing, "Glo-ry, glo-ry,

hal-le-lu-jah! He reigns, ___ He reigns!" All God's chil-dren sing-ing,

"Glo-ry, glo-ry, hal-le-lu-jah! He reigns!" ___

HERE I AM TO WORSHIP

Words and Music by
TIM HUGHES

Moderately

Light of the world, You stepped out into darkness, opened my eyes, let me see. Beauty that made this heart adore You, hope of a life spent with You.

© 2001 THANKYOU MUSIC (PRS)
Admin. Worldwide excluding the UK and Europe by WORSHIPTOGETHER.COM SONGS
Admin. in the UK and Europe by KINGSWAY MUSIC
All Rights Reserved   Used by Permission

Here I am to worship; here I am to bow down; here I am to say that You're my God. You're altogether lovely, altogether worthy, altogether wonderful to me.

King of all days, oh, so highly exalted,

glor-i-ous in heav-en a-bove, hum-bly You came to the earth You cre-at-ed, all for love's sake be-came poor. Here I am to wor-ship; here I am to bow down; here I am to say that You're my God. You're al-to-geth-er love-ly, al-to-geth-er worthy, altogether wonderful to me. And I'll never know how much it cost to see my sin upon that cross. I'll never know how much it cost to see my sin upon that cross. And I'll never know how much

it cost to see my sin upon that cross. And I'll never know how much it cost to see my sin upon that cross. Here I am to worship; here I am to bow down; here I am to say that You're my God.
(Here I am.)
You're al - to - geth - er

lovely, al - to - geth - er wor - thy, al - to - geth - er won - der - ful to me.

Here I am to won - der - ful to me.
(me.)

Repeat and Fade

Optional Ending

LIVING HALLELUJAH

Words and Music by
SARAH KELLY

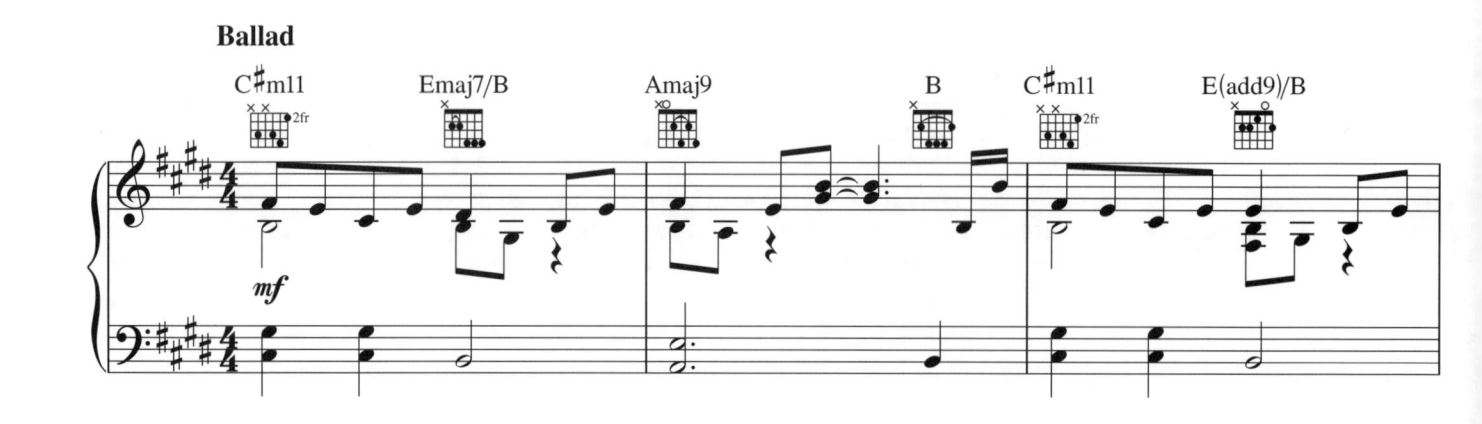

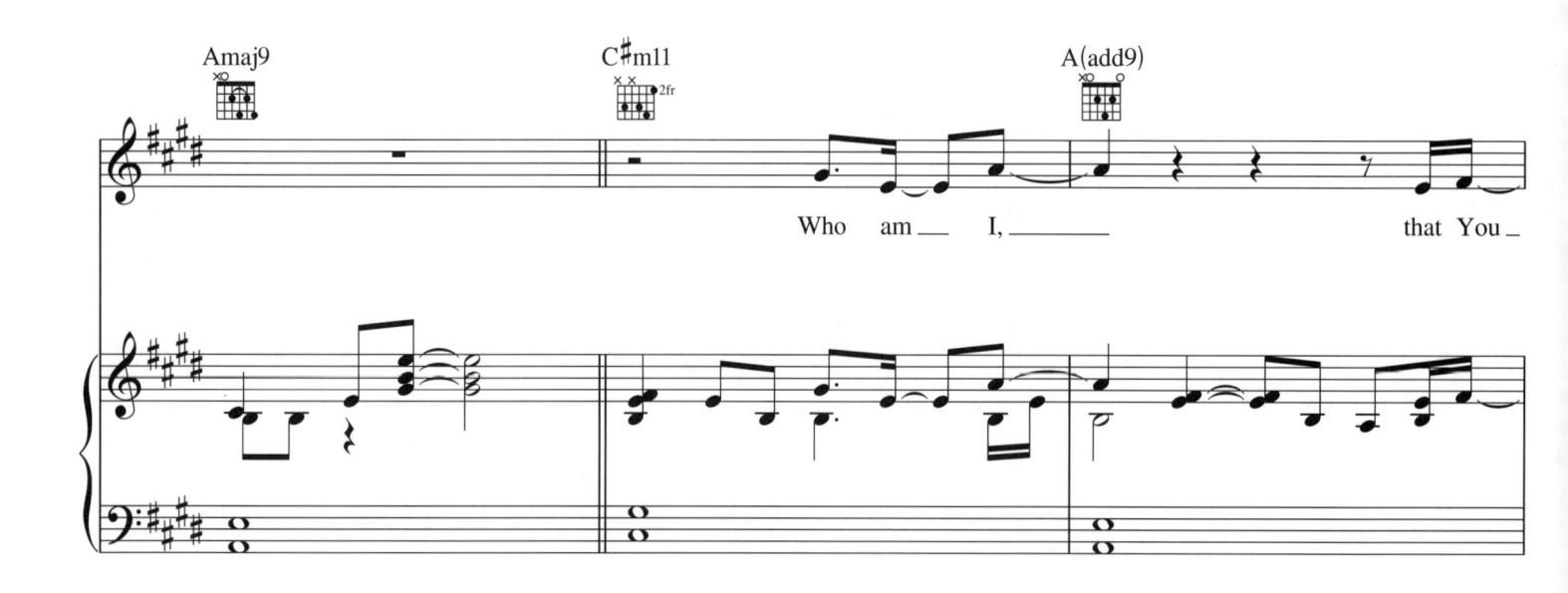

Ballad

Who am I, that You came to Earth for me to die on a tree?

© 2003 EMACK MUSIC (ASCAP), MEADOWGREEN MUSIC (ASCAP) and SARAH KELLY MUSIC (ASCAP)
Admin. by EMI CMG PUBLISHING
All Rights Reserved   Used by Permission

And who are You? Son of man, son of God, yes, I believe it's true. More than words I bring to You. May all I say and may all I do be hallelujah, hallelujah.

Lyrics:

May ev'ry-thing about me be halle-lujah to my king. Halle-lu-jah, halle-lu-jah. May ev'ry-thing about me be halle-lu-jah.

C♯m9
E/B
Amaj9
C♯m11
E(add9)/B
Amaj9
C♯m11
A(add9)
E(add9)
All of me I surren - der complete-
B(add9)
C♯m11
A(add9)
- ly. Take con - trol. I want
E(add9)
B(add9)
all of You, and I'm let - ting go.
2fr
7fr

I am healed and I'm for-giv-en.

I am free be-cause I'm liv-ing hal-le-lu-jah, hal-le-lu-jah.

May ev-'ry-thing a-bout me be hal-le-

E(add9)/B
A♭7/C
E(add9)
lu - jah to my king. Hal - le - lu - jah,
B
A♭7♭9/C
3fr
C♯m7
4fr
C♯m7/B
9fr
hal - le - lu - jah. May
3
A(add9)
E
ev - 'ry - thing a - bout me be hal - le -
A(add9)
Bsus
B
E
Asus2
E
- lu - jah.

B(add4)   **C#m7**

And it's all so clear, and it's all so clear,

F#7   **Asus2**   **E**

I was born to wor - ship.

B(add4)   **C#m7**

And it's all so clear, and it's all so clear,

F#7   **A(add9)**   **B**

I was born to wor - ship. Hal - le -

-lu - jah, _____ hal - le - lu - jah. _____

May ev - 'ry - thing __ a - bout __ me be __ hal - le -

-lu - jah. _____ Hal - le -

-lu - jah. _____

LOST IN WONDER

Words and Music by
MARTYN LAYZELL

chose the cross with ev-'ry breath; the per-fect life, the per-fect death.
loosed the cords of sin-ful-ness, and broke the chains of my dis-grace.

You chose the cross.
You chose the cross.

crown of thorns __ You wore for us, __ and crowned us with __ e - ter - nal life.
from the grace __ vic - to - ri - ous, __ You rose a - gain __ so glo - ri - ous.

You chose __ the cross. __ And
You chose __ the cross. __ The

though Your soul __ was o - ver - whelmed __ with pain, __ o -
sor - row that __ sur - round - ed You __ was mine, __ yet,

be - di - ent __ to death, __ You o - ver - came.
"Not My will, __ but Yours __ be done," You __ cried.

I'm lost in

B♭ Gm7 E♭sus2
wonder, I'm lost in love, I'm lost in praise for evermore.
F Fsus F B♭ Gm7
Because of Jesus' unfailing love, I am for-
E♭sus2 To Coda 1 F 2 F
given, I am restored. You
Fsus Cm7 B♭/D Fsus F
And though Your soul was overwhelmed with pain, o-

be - di - ent __ to death, __ You o - ver - came. __ The sor - row that __ sur - round - ed You __ was mine, __ yet, "Not my will, __ but Yours __ be done," __ You __ cried. I'm lost in

D.S. al Coda

CODA

Be - cause of Je - sus, __ be - cause of Je - sus, __ be - cause of

E♭sus2
6fr
Fsus
F
B♭
Je - sus I am re-stored. Be-cause of Je - sus, be-cause of
Gm7
E♭sus2
6fr
Je - sus, be-cause of Je - sus I am re-stored.
F
Fsus
F
B♭
I'm lost in won - der, I'm lost in
Gm7
E♭sus2
6fr
love, I'm lost in praise for - ev - er - more.

Be - cause of Jesus' un - fail - ing love, I am for - giv - en, I am re - stored. Be - cause of Je - sus, be - cause of Je - sus, be - cause of Je - sus. Be - cause of Je - sus, be - cause of

Je - sus, ___ be - cause of Je - sus ___

I'm re - stored. __

(Vocal ad lib.)

And I'm for - giv - en. _____

Repeat ad lib. | **Final Ending**

SPIRIT

Words and Music by
JONATHAN FOREMAN

Flowing

Spir - it, fall fresh on me.
Spir - it, come be my joy.

© 1999 MEADOWGREEN MUSIC (ASCAP) and SUGAR PETE SONGS (ASCAP)
Admin. by EMI CMG PUBLISHING
All Rights Reserved   Used by Permission

Spir - it, fall fresh on me.
Spir - it, come be my joy.

Cmaj7   Dsus

G   Dm

Hear my cry,
Be my song,

Am7   C   Dsus

fill my life.
fill my lungs.

I won't need anything _____ but You. _____ I've found all that I _____ want, _____ all that I _____ long _____ for in You. _____ I've found

all that I want, all that I long for in You. And wasted time is when I'm far from Your truth. I've found all that I ___ want, ___ all that I ___ long ___ for ___ in

You.

for ___ in You. _____

I've found all that I want, all that I long

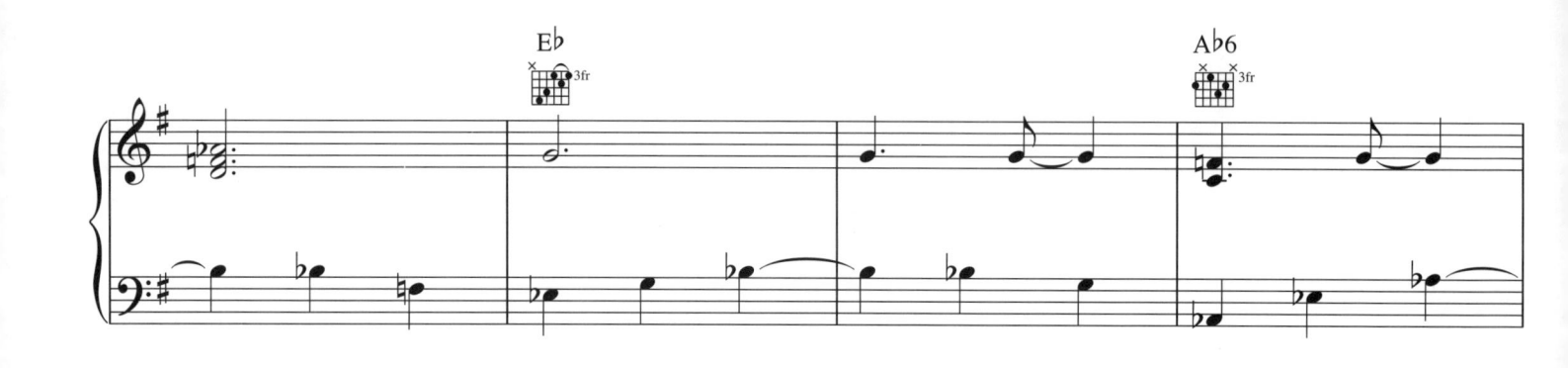

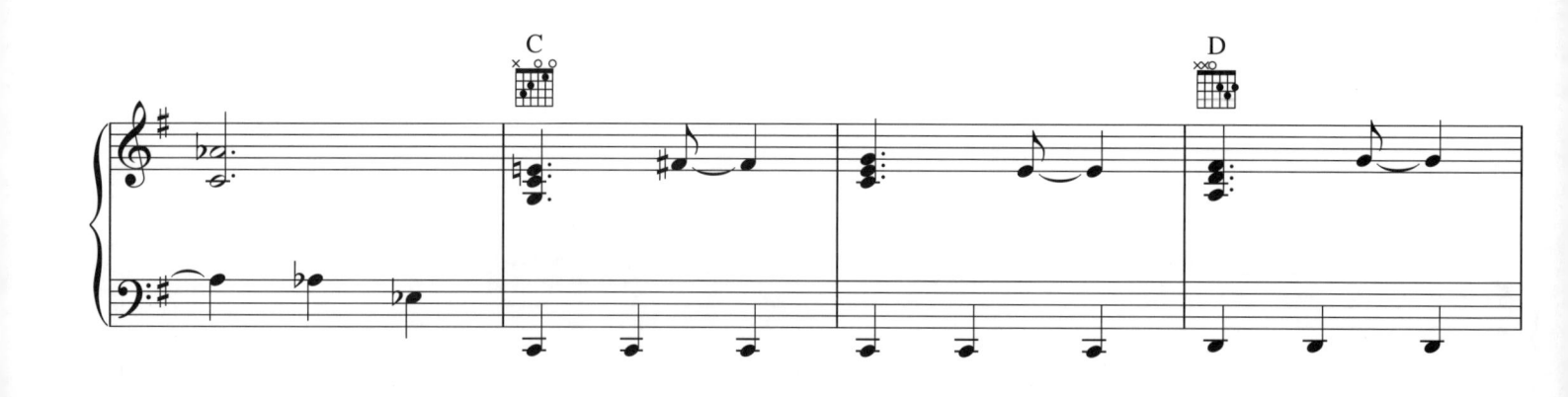

for in You.

I've found all that I want, all that I long

for in You.

So, wasted time

Em7
Csus2
3fr
is when I'm far from Your truth.
A7
C
I've found all that I want, and all that I long
Dsus
G
for. And all that I want,
Em7
Csus2
3fr
all that I long for {in / is} You.

107

NO ONE LIKE YOU

Words and Music by JACK PARKER, MIKE DODSON, JASON SOLLEY, MIKE HOGAN, JEREMY BUSH and DAVID CROWDER

Joyfully

You are more beau-ti-ful than an-y-one ev-er.

Ev-'ry day You're the same. You nev-er change, no, nev-er.

*Recorded a half step lower.

© 2003 WORSHIPTOGETHER.COM SONGS (ASCAP), sixsteps Music (ASCAP) and INOT MUSIC (ASCAP)
WORSHIPTOGETHER.COM SONGS and sixsteps Music Admin. by EMI CMG PUBLISHING
All Rights Reserved   Used by Permission

You are more beautiful than anyone ever.

Ev-'ry day You're the same. You nev-er change, no, nev-er.

G Em7 Dsus Csus2
And how could I ev - er de - ny the love of my Sav - ior?
G Em7 Dsus Csus2
You are to me ev - 'ry - thing, all I need for - ev - er.
D5 Em Csus2 G D
How could You be so good? There is
Em7 Csus2 G D Em7 C
no one like You. There has nev - er ev - er been an - y - one _ like You.

111

How could You be so good to me? E-ter-nal-ly, I be-lieve.

There is no one like You. There has nev-er ev-er been an-y-one like You.

ev-er been an-y-one like You,

You, You, You, You, You, You.

G
Dsus
Em7
Csus2
3fr
D5
5fr
Csus2
3fr
Dsus
Csus2
3fr
How could You be so good to me?
Dsus
Csus2
3fr
We're not a - lone, so sing a - long.
Dsus
Csus2
3fr
We're not a - lone, so sing a - long,

sing a - long, sing a - long.

G **D** **Em7** **Csus2**
There is no one like You.

G **D** **Em7** **C**
There has nev - er ev - er been an - y - one like You.

N.C.
There is no one like You.

115

There has nev-er ev-er been an-y-one like You.

There is no one like You.

1. There has nev-er ev-er been an-y-one like You.

2. ev-er been. There is no one like our God.

RAIN DOWN

Words and Music by MARTIN SMITH
and STUART GARRARD

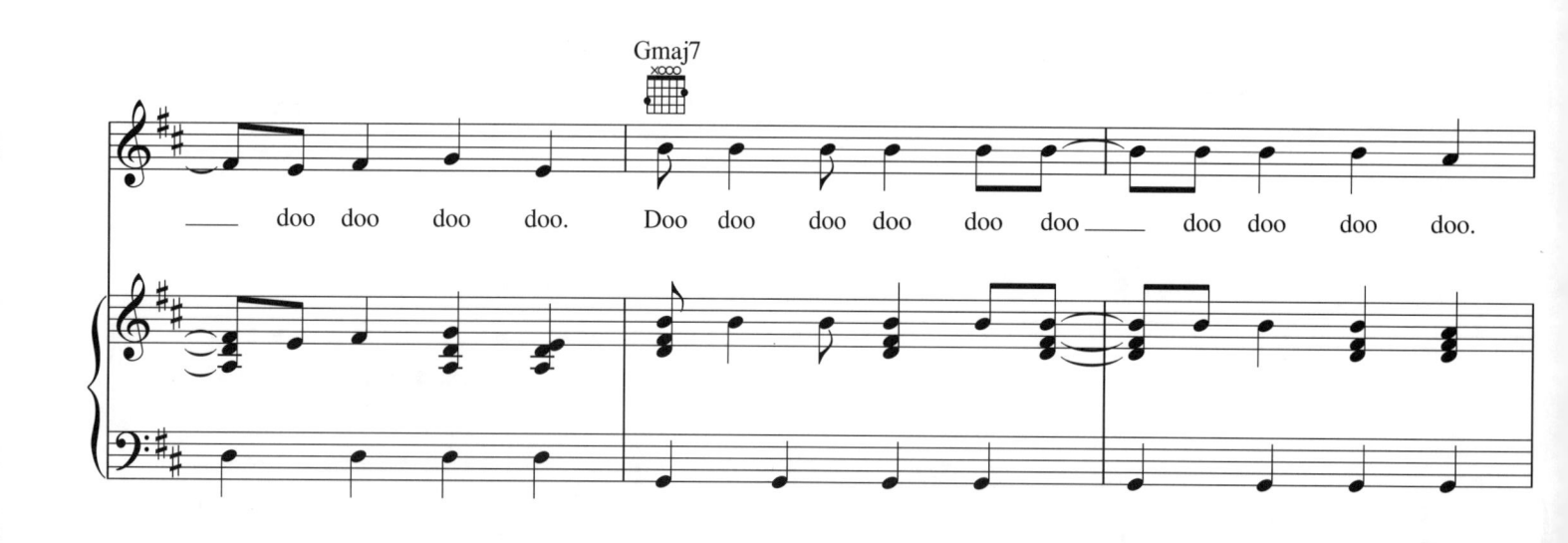

Moderately fast

Doo doo doo doo doo doo doo doo doo doo. Doo doo doo doo doo doo doo doo doo doo. Doo doo doo doo. Doo doo doo doo doo doo doo doo doo doo. Doo doo doo doo doo doo doo doo.

© 2003 CURIOUS? MUSIC (PRS)
Admin. in the U.S. and Canada by BIRDWING MUSIC, a d/b/a of EMI CMG PUBLISHING
All Rights Reserved   Used by Permission

Looks like to - night ___ the sky ___ is heav -
my heart ___ is heav -

y.
y. Feels like the winds ___
Feels like it's time ___

D
G
are gon - na change.
to dream a - gain.
Be - neath my feet
I see the clouds,
Bm
D
G
the earth is read - y.
and yes, I'm read - y
Bm
D
I know it's time
to dance up - on
for heav - en's rain.
this bar - ren land,
G
D
It's gon - na rain,
hope in my hands,

119

all a-round the world we're sing-ing. Rain down; can you hear the earth is sing-ing? Rain down; my heart is dry, but still I'm sing-ing. Rain down.

121

o-pen ___ up, o-pen ___ up, o-pen ___ up our ___ hearts. ___ Rain down; all a-round __ the world __ we're sing-ing.

123

D
Give me strength to cross this water. Keep my feet, don't let

Gmaj7 **G**
me fal-ter. Rain down.

Gmaj7 **G** **Bm**
Do not

D **Gmaj7**
shut the heav-ens, but o-

-pen up our hearts, o-pen up our hearts.

Do not shut the heav-ens, but o-pen up our hearts, o-pen up our hearts.

SALVATION

Words and Music by
CHARLIE HALL

With excitement, in 2

Sal - va - tion, spring up from the ground, Lord, rend the heav - ens and come down, seek the lost and heal the lame; Je - sus bring glo - ry to Your name. Let all the

© 2000 WORSHIPTOGETHER.COM SONGS (ASCAP) and sixsteps Music (ASCAP)
Admin. by EMI CMG PUBLISHING
All Rights Reserved   Used by Permission

prod-i-gals run home, all of cre-a-tion waits and groans. Lord, we've heard

of Your great fame; Father, cause all to shout Your name.

Stir up our hearts, ___ oh ___ God; ___

o - pen our spir - its to awe ___ who You are. ___

Put a cry ___ in ___ us so ___ deep ___

___ in - side that we can - not find the ___ words ___

129

Sal - va - tion, spring up from the ground, Lord, rend the heav - ens and come down, seek the lost and heal the lame; Je - sus bring glo - ry to Your name. Let all the prod - i - gals run home, all of cre - a - tion waits and groans.

Lord, we've heard of Your great fame; Fa-ther, cause all to shout Your name.

Repeat and Fade | **Optional Ending**

SING TO THE KING

Words and Music by
BILLY JAMES FOOTE

With praise

(1., 2.) Sing to the King who is coming to reign. Glory to Jesus, the Lamb that was slain.
(3.) For His returning we watch and we pray. We will be ready the dawn of that day.

© 2003 WORSHIPTOGETHER.COM SONGS (ASCAP) and sixsteps Music (ASCAP)
Admin. by EMI CMG PUBLISHING
All Rights Reserved   Used by Permission

Life and sal - va - tion His em - pire shall bring,
We'll join in sing - ing with all the re - deemed,
and joy to the na - tions when
'cause Sa - tan is van - quished and
Je - sus is King.
Je - sus is King.
1
2, 3
Come, let us sing a song, a

song de-claring that we belong to Jesus.

Oh, and He is all we need,

yeah, yeah. Oh, lift up a heart of praise.

Sing now with voices raised to Jesus, oh.

135

To Coda E

Sing to the King.

E5 **D.S. al Coda**

CODA E

King.

Oh, just sing to the King, sing to the

King.

SONG OF LOVE

Words and Music by REBECCA ST. JAMES,
MATT BRONLEEWE and JEREMY ASH

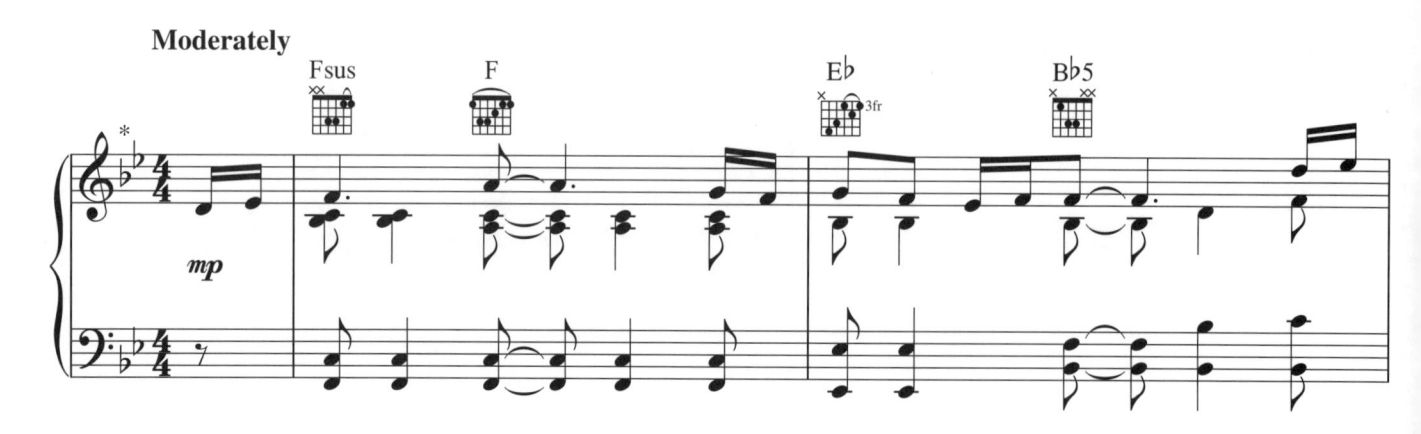

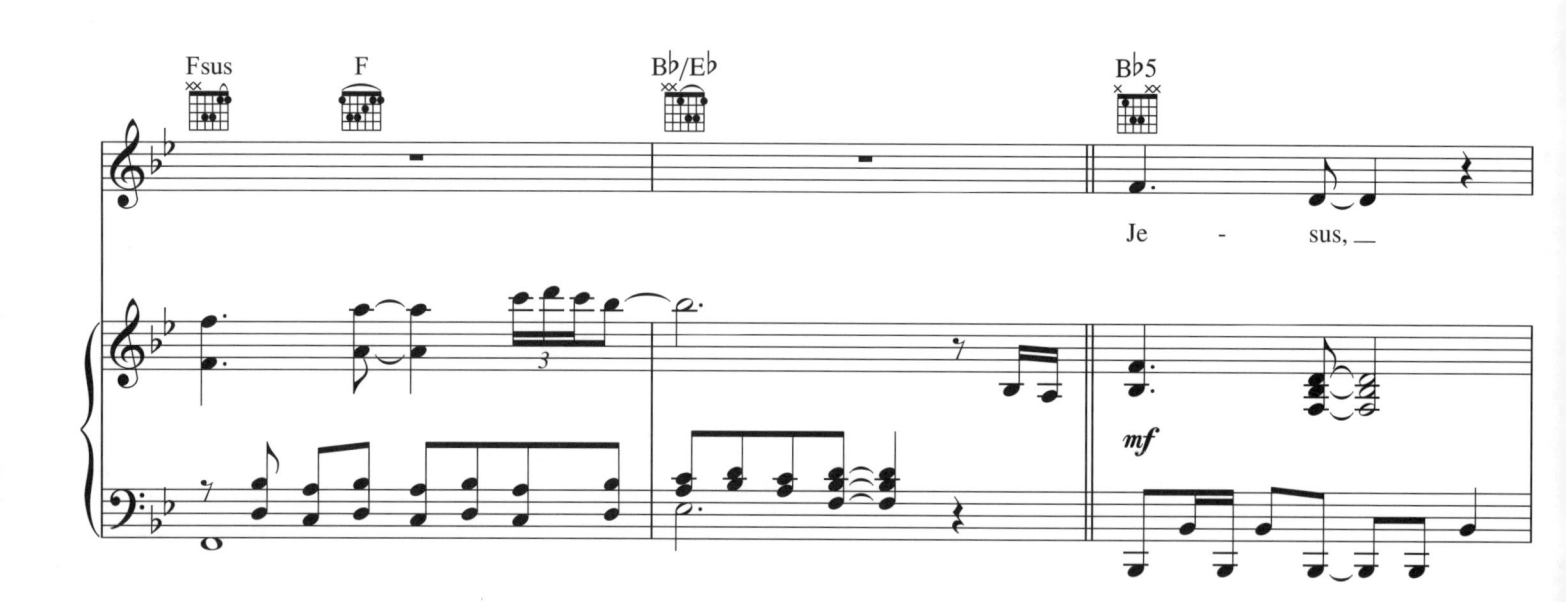

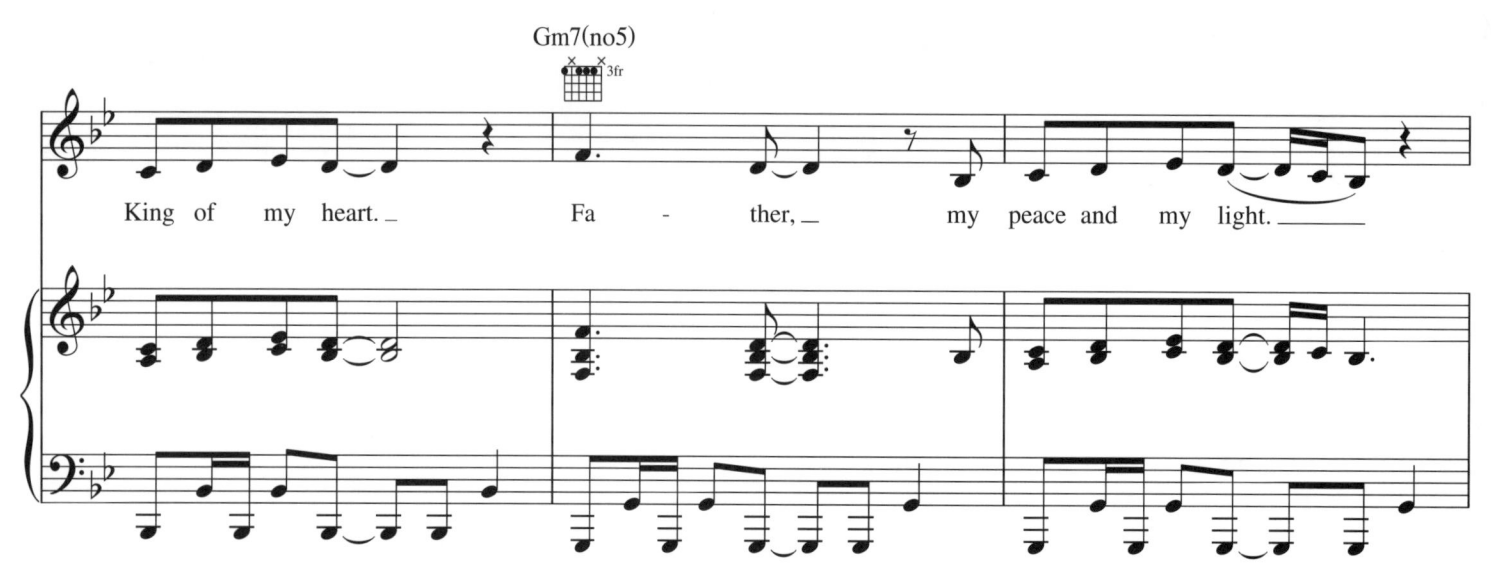

*Recorded a half step higher.

© 2002 UP IN THE MIX MUSIC (BMI), BIBBITSONG MUSIC (BMI), SONGS OF WINDSWEPT PACIFIC (BMI), SONGS FROM THE FARM (BMI),
MUSIC OF WINDSWEPT (ASCAP), GRANGE ROAD MUSIC (ASCAP), TYPICAL HITS (ASCAP) and PROJECT 76 MUSIC (ASCAP)
UP IN THE MIX MUSIC Admin. by EMI CMG PUBLISHING
BIBBITSONG MUSIC Admin. by ICG
GRANGE ROAD MUSIC, TYPICAL HITS and PROJECT 76 MUSIC Admin. by MUSIC OF WINDSWEPT
SONGS FROM THE FARM Admin. by SONGS OF WINDSWEPT PACIFIC
All Rights Reserved   Used by Permission

137

heav - ens ___ de - clare You are God, ___ and the
moun - tains __ re - joice. ___ The o - ceans __ cry
"Al - le - lu - ia" __ as we wor - ship __ You, Lord, __ for
this is our song _ of love. __

139

heav - ens ___ de - clare You are God, ___ and the moun - tains ___ re - joice. __

The o - ceans ___ cry "Al - le - lu - ia" ___ as we

1.
wor - ship ___ You, Lord. _____ The

2.
wor - ship ___ You, Lord, _____ as we

Fsus/C
B♭maj7/D
3fr
E♭sus2
6fr
wor - ship You, Lord,
for this is our song of love.
dim.
B♭5
Gm7(no5)
3fr
mp
Our song of love,
E♭sus2
6fr
our song of love;
Repeat and Fade
F5
this is our song of love.
B♭5
Optional Ending
F5
B♭5
this is our song of love.

SPIRIT WALTZ

Words and Music by
ERIC OWYOUNG

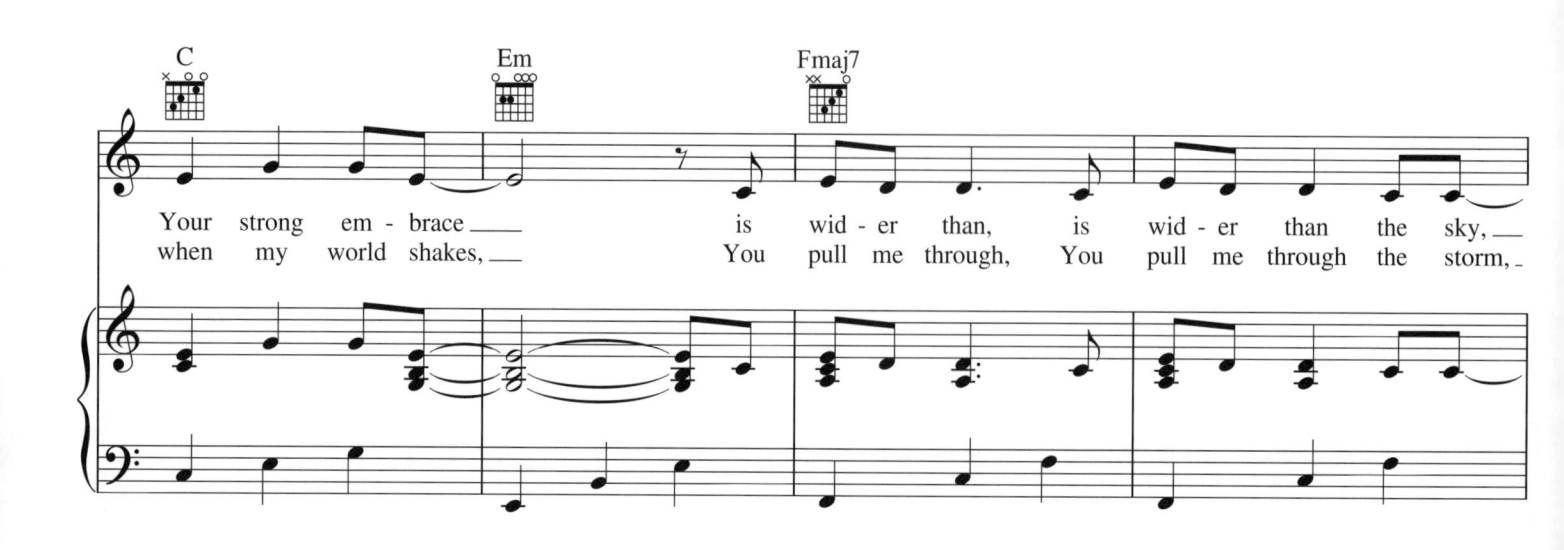

Slow Waltz

Your cup of grace ___ is deep-er than, is deep-er than the o-
Your per-fect words ___ go fur-ther than, go fur-ther than to-mor-

-cean, ___ yeah. ___
-row, ___ yeah. ___ And

Your strong em-brace ___ is wid-er than, is wid-er than the sky, ___
when my world shakes, ___ You pull me through, You pull me through the storm, __

© 2004 BIRDWING MUSIC (ASCAP)
Admin. by EMI CMG PUBLISHING
All Rights Reserved   Used by Permission

yeah.
yeah.

Je - sus, my heart can - not break e - nough for

Your love, a well that runs

144

145

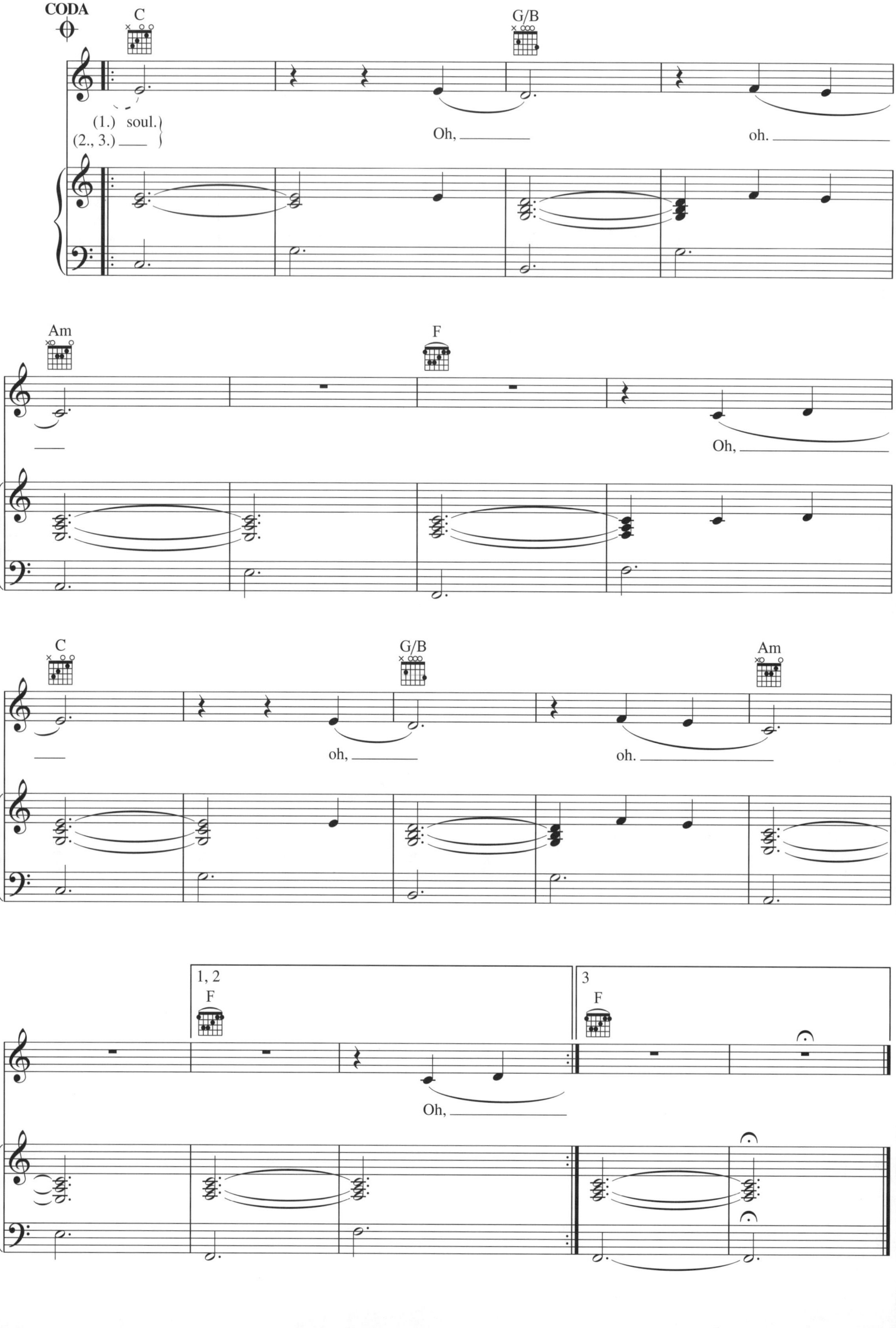
CODA
C
G/B
(1.) soul.
(2., 3.)
Oh,
oh.
Am
F
Oh,
C
G/B
Am
oh,
oh.
1, 2
F
3
F
Oh,

TAKE MY LIFE

Words and Music by CHRIS TOMLIN
and LOUIE GIGLIO

Gently

Take my life and let it be consecrated, Lord, to Thee.
Take my voice and let me sing always, only, for my King.
Take my will and make it Thine, it shall be no longer mine.

Take my moments and my days, let them flow in cease-
Take my lips and let them be filled with mes-sag-es
Take my heart, it is Thine own, it shall be Thy roy-

© 2003 WORSHIPTOGETHER.COM SONGS (ASCAP) and sixsteps Music (ASCAP)
Admin. by EMI CMG PUBLISHING
All Rights Reserved Used by Permission

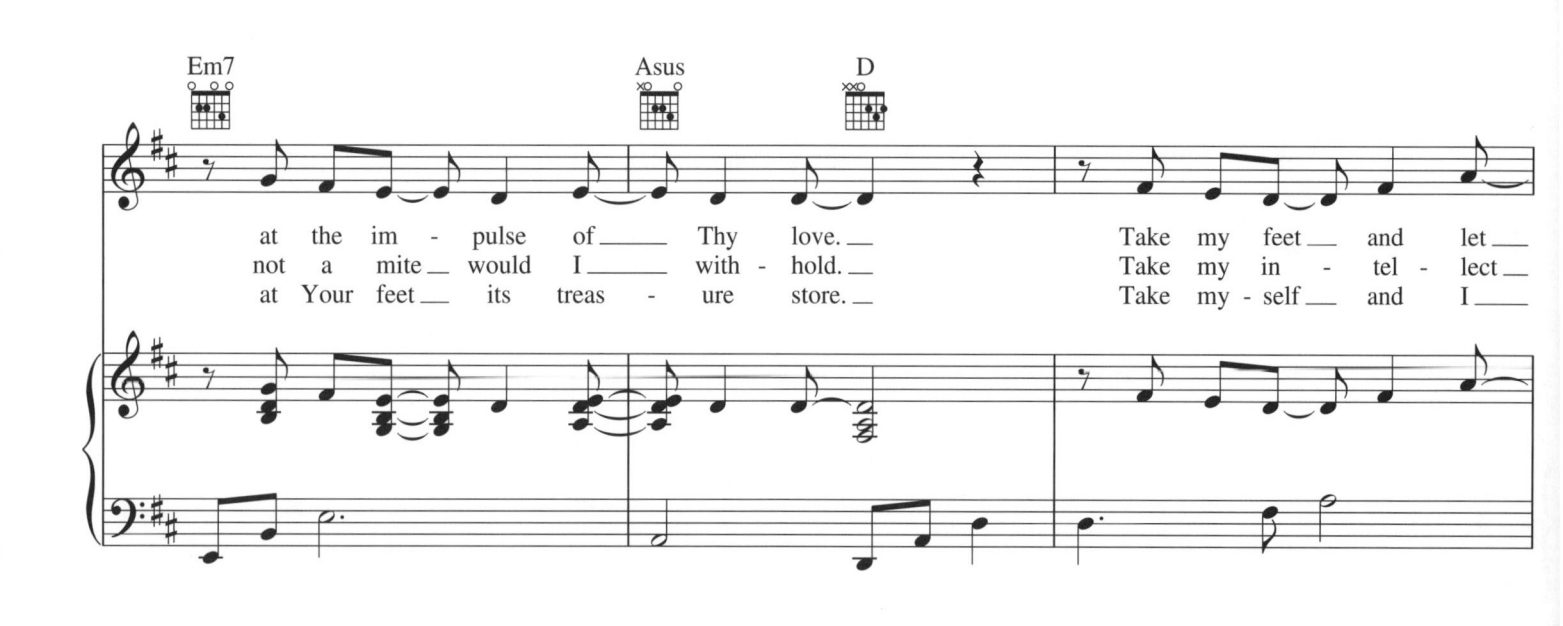

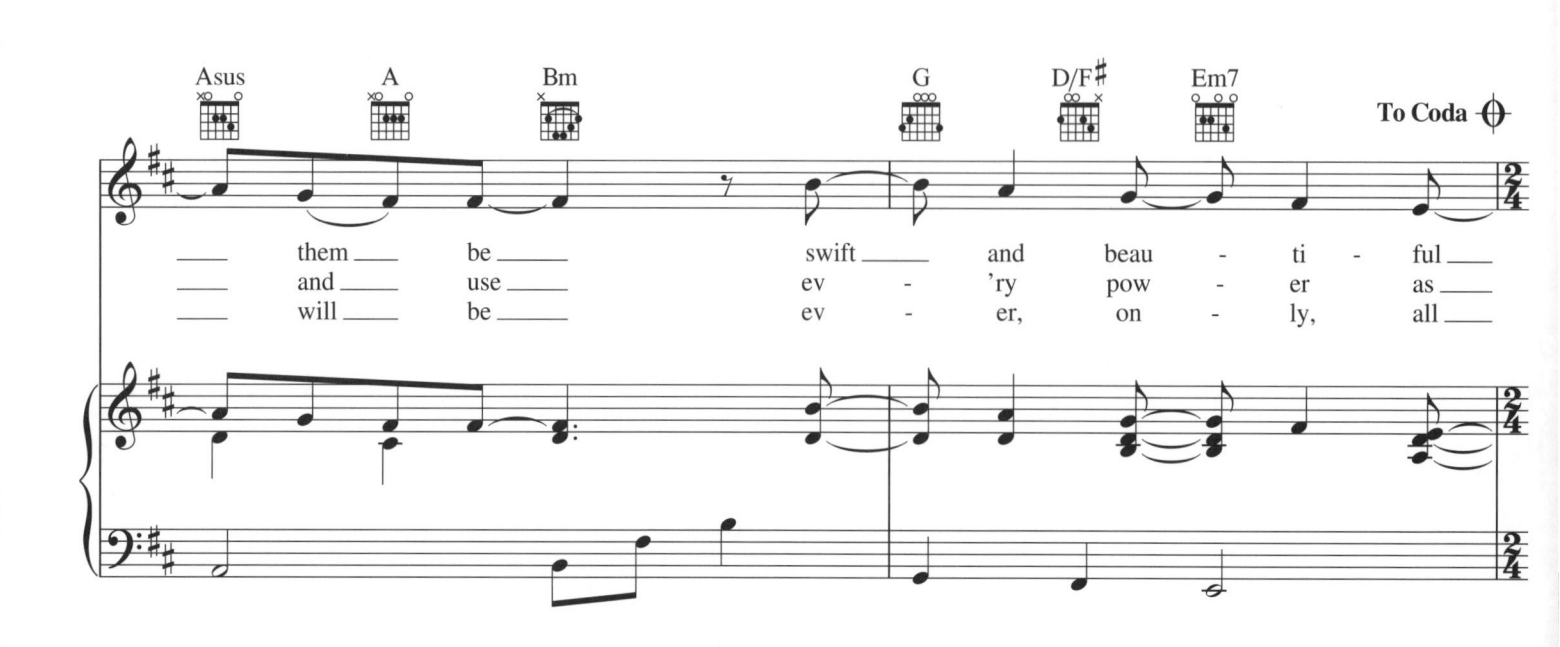

less praise. Take my hands and let them move
from Thee. Take my sil - ver and my gold,
al throne. Take my love, my Lord, I pour

at the im - pulse of Thy love. Take my feet and let
not a mite would I with - hold. Take my in - tel - lect
at Your feet its treas - ure store. Take my - self and I

them be swift and beau - ti - ful
and use ev - 'ry pow - er as
will be ev - er, on - ly, all

Asus
Dsus2
1
for Thee.
You choose.
2
Em7
Gsus2
Here am I,
all of me.
Asus
Em7
Take my life,
Gsus2
Asus
D.S. al Coda
it's all for Thee.

CODA
Asus
D
Asus
A
Bm
for Thee.
Take my - self and I will be ev -
G
D/F♯
Em7
Asus
D
- er, on - ly, all for Thee.
Em7
D/F♯
Gsus2
Here am I, all of me.
mf
Asus
Em7
D/F♯
Take my life,

151

Stronger Than The Storm

Words and Music by
VICKY BEECHING

Moderately fast

When we're soaked by the rain of sor- row,
With one word You can calm the o- cean, when we're bat- turn- ing cha-

© 2004 THANKYOU MUSIC (PRS)
Admin. Worldwide excluding the UK and Europe by WORSHIPTOGETHER.COM SONGS
Admin. in the UK and Europe by KINGSWAY MUSIC
All Rights Reserved   Used by Permission

-tered by winds of change,
-os to glass-like seas.

when the world all a-round is shak-in',
Speak un-shak-a-ble hope to our hearts.

and we're deaf-ened by crash-ing
Be our for-tress of per-fect

waves, we call out
peace. We will trust

to You, ___ to You. ___
in You, ___ in You. } You are __ strong-

-er ___ than ___ the ___ storm. ___

You are __ reign - ing ___ o - ver ___ all. ___

Faith - ful God, You're __

155

You'll turn the darkness into dawn. We'll feel the sunlight's healing warmth once more. You are stronger than the storm, yes, You are. You are reign-ing o-ver all.

Faith-ful God, You're al-ways in con-trol, 'cause You are strong-er than the storm. You are reigning over all.

Faithful God, You're always in control. You're the anchor of peace, You're the an - chor of peace, You're the an - chor of peace for our souls. (You will turn the dark - ness in - to dawn.) You're in con - trol. (You're strong - er than the storm.)

WE BOW DOWN

Words and Music by
TWILA PARIS

Moderately, in 1

161

Lyrics:
(Lord/King) of cre-a-tion and (Lord/King) of my life, (Lord/King) of the land and the sea. You were (Lord/King) of the heav-ens before there was time, and (Lord/King) of all (lords/kings) You will be. We bow down and we

E
A
Dsus
wor - ship You, Lord.
crown You the King.
We bow down and we
E
A
Dsus
wor - ship You, Lord.
crown You the King.
We bow down and we
E
F#m7
Bm11
Esus
wor - ship You, Lord.
crown You the King.
Lord
King
of all
lords
kings
You will
1
A
E/G#
D/A
A
be.

163

We bow down _____ and we wor-ship You, _____ Lord. We bow down _____ and we wor-ship You, _____ Lord. We bow down _____ and we wor-ship You, _____ Lord. Lord of all lords _____ You will

1
C(add4)
be. We bow
2
C
G(add4)/B
be.
F/C
C
G(add4)/B
F/C
C
G(add4)/B
F/C
(We bow down, we bow down.)
C
G(add4)/B
F/A
Fsus2
(We bow down, we bow down.)

WONDERFUL MAKER

Words and Music by MATT REDMAN
and CHRIS TOMLIN

Moderately

You spread out the skies over empty space.

Said, "Let there be light," and to a dark and formless world Your light was born.

© 2002 THANKYOU MUSIC (PRS), WORSHIPTOGETHER.COM SONGS (ASCAP) and sixsteps Music (ASCAP)
THANKYOU MUSIC Admin. Worldwide excluding the UK and Europe by WORSHIPTOGETHER.COM SONGS
THANKYOU MUSIC Admin. in the UK and Europe by KINGSWAY MUSIC
WORSHIPTOGETHER.COM SONGS and sixsteps Music Admin. by EMI CMG PUBLISHING
All Rights Reserved   Used by Permission

Db(add9)

You spread out Your arms over empty hearts.

Fm7

Said, "Let there be light," and to a dark and hopeless world Your Son was born.

Db(add9)   **Ebsus2**

You

Bbm7   **Ab/C**   **Db(add9)**

made the world and saw that it was good. You

sent Your on-ly Son for You are ____ good.

What a won-der-ful Mak - er. What a won-der-ful Sav-

-ior. How maj-est-ic Your whis - pers

and how hum-ble Your love. ____

With a strength like no oth - er and the heart of a Fa - ther, how maj - est - ic Your whis - pers.

What a won - der - ful God.

No eye has ful - ly seen how

beau - ti - ful the cross. And we have on - ly heard the

faint - est whis - pers of how great You are.

You

You made the world and saw that it was good. You

171

sent Your on-ly Son for You are good.

CODA
What a won-der-ful God.

How maj-est-ic Your whis-pers.

What a won-der-ful God.

YAHWEH

Words and Music by
SHAWN McDONALD

Moderately

You a - lone are wor - thy.

© 2004 BIRDWING MUSIC (ASCAP) and SHAWN MCDONALD MUSIC (ASCAP)
Admin. by EMI CMG PUBLISHING
All Rights Reserved   Used by Permission

Gsus2
You a - lone are
Gsus
3fr
G
wor - thy
of all that I am,
C6
of all that I am.
G
To Coda
1

Beau - ti - ful is Your name, beau - ti - ful is Your name, Yah - weh.

D.S. al Coda

You alone are worthy.

You alone are worthy of all that I am.